Tractors

by Peter Brady

Bridgestone Books

an Imprint of Capstone Press

Bridgestone Books are published by Capstone Press
818 North Willow Street, Mankato, Minnesota 56001
Copyright © 1996 by Capstone Press
Printed in the United States of America

Library of Congress Cataloging-in-Publication Data
Brady, Peter. 1944–
      Tractors/Peter Brady
      p. cm.
      Includes bibliographical references and index.
      Summary: In brief text, describes the many ways that farmers use tractors in the growing
      of crops.
      ISBN 1-56065-348-5
      1. Farm tractors--Juvenile literature. [1. Tractors. 2. Agricultural machinery.] I. Title.
TL233.15.B73 1996
631.3'72--dc20

                                        95-47767
                                          CIP
                                          AC

Photo credits
Peter Ford: cover, 4-10, 14, 18
Joe Staudenbaur: 12, 16, 20

9.95

Table of Contents

Farmers Use Tractors 5

The Cab 7

The Tires 9

The Engine 11

The Power Takeoff 13

Breaking Up the Soil 15

Planting and Cultivating 17

Spreaders and Sprayers 19

Other Equipment 21

Hands On: Plant Your Own Crops 22

Words to Know 23

Read More 24

Index 24

Words in **boldface** type in the text are defined in the Words to Know section in the back of this book.

Farmers Use Tractors

Farmers use tractors to plant crops. They use them to take care of the crops while they are growing. Tractors are used for many **chores** around the farm, too.

The Cab

Many tractors have a cab. A cab covers the driver's seat. A cab has a heater for cold weather. It has an air conditioner for hot weather.

The Tires

Tractor tires have deep grooves called lugs. Lugs help tires go through mud and water without getting stuck. Some tractors have **duals** for even more grip.

The Engine

Tractor engines are powerful, but they are not fast. They do not use much fuel. Farmers keep track of an engine's hours rather than its miles.

The Power Takeoff

Some equipment needs to get power from the tractor. Farmers hook this equipment to the power takeoff. The power takeoff is a metal pole that gets power from the tractor's engine.

Breaking Up the Soil

Farmers use tractors to pull plows and harrows. The plow breaks the ground into chunks. The harrow breaks those chunks into smaller ones. These tools make the soil ready for planting.

Planting and Cultivating

Tractors pull planters and cultivators. The planter puts crop seeds into the ground. After the crops start to grow, the cultivator digs up weeds that grow between the rows.

Spreaders and Sprayers

Tractors pull **manure** spreaders that **fertilize** the ground. The spreaders are hooked up to the power takeoff. Sprayers spray **pesticides** to kill insects and diseases. Spreaders and sprayers attach to the tractor rather than being pulled by it.

Other Equipment

Tractors pull mowers that cut hay and straw. They pull swath turners that turn over hay and straw so it dries. After the hay and straw dries, tractors pull balers that wrap the hay and straw into bundles called bales.

Hands On: Plant Your Own Crops

1. Fill a cake pan with soil from your backyard. Dark soil works best. You can also buy soil from a plant store.
2. Use a fork to plow and harrow the soil. Breaking up the soil makes it ready for planting seeds.
3. Plant bean seeds in rows about one inch (about 2.5 centimeters) apart.
4. Put the pan where it will get plenty of sunlight. Keep the pan at room temperature.
5. Give your crops about half a glass of water once a day.
6. You have done the work of a tractor. Watch your crops grow.

Words to Know

chores—the many small tasks a farmer does

duals—two rear tires on each side of a tractor

fertilize—putting things in the soil to make it better for growing

manure—animal waste that fertilizes soil

pesticides—chemicals used to kill insects or weeds

Read More

Brown, Craig McFarland. *Tractor.* New York: Greenwillow Books, 1995.

Gibbons, Gail. *Farming.* New York: Holiday House, 1988.

Llewellyn, Claire. *Tractor.* New York: Dorling Kindersley, 1995.

Young, Caroline. *The Usborne Book of Tractors.* Tulsa, Okla.:EDC, 1992.

Index

air conditioner, 7
balers, 21
bales, 21
cabs, 7
chores, 5
cultivators, 17
duals, 9
fertilize, 19
harrows, 15
hay, 21

manure spreaders, 19
mowers, 21
pesticides, 19
planters, 17
plows, 15
power takeoff, 13, 19
seeds, 17, 22
soil, 15, 22
straw, 21
weeds, 17